NEVER A $7 WH*RE

Toni Crowe

Editing: Nerdy WordSmith
Cover Art: Nina Z
Formatting: Polgarus Studio

Do you have trouble distinguishing good relationships from bad relationships? Unsure if you are in a relationship that is horrific for you but great for your significant other? You need "The Relationship Thermometer Checklist" to assess your relationship.

I fell blindly in love when I was eighteen and ran away with a pimp. I was in a one-sided relationship, but I was in too deep to see the truth until it was almost too late. I should have known that my lover was only using me.

Do you need to assess your relationship? I have prepared a relationship checklist of the questions I should have asked myself. Use this checklist to assist you in determining if your current relationship is toxic. Go to the link below to receive "The Relationship Thermometer Checklist."

Authors' Note

*NEVER a $7 Wh*re* is the true-crime experience I had moving from Chicago to Cleveland with a pimp while I was still a teenager. It is the first of four books I've written about my life. The second, *The Daytime Lives of the Ladies of the Night*, detailed the daylight lives of the escorts I lived with. The third, *Bullets and Bosses Don't Have Friends*, my corporate career and the fourth was the workbook for the third. The fifth book will convey how I have managed to stay in a passionate and loving relationship for 40 years.

I am unusual in that most women who are targeted for the whore life never escape. I not only escaped but thrived. People's names have been changed to protect their anonymity; some, in their old age, have gone straight. Others I have given a pseudonym to further obscure their identity. I have deliberately hidden the location of the home where I lived in Cleveland and the places where I worked.

Bill, you are my strength. Sean and Tamara, you are my inspiration. Alyssa, Anthony, and Lyriah, you are my joy. All I do I do for love . . . and money, but mostly love.

You gain strength, courage, and confidence by every experience in which you stop to look fear in the face. You are able to say to yourself, "I lived through this horror. I can take the next thing that comes along."

Eleanor Roosevelt

Contents

Chapter 1
Introduction

> "I learned how to comport myself among trolls, elves, hobbits, or goblins. I learned that a friend can be lost to greed and avarice, I learned that solving riddles may be as important a survival skill as bowmanship. I know how to talk to a dragon, and that it is best not to." – Karen Joy Fowler

The simplest fact of life is that every person in the world makes mistakes.

But no mistake needs to be unrecoverable. No person deserves to have their life pushed off track by one poor decision, their entire life affected by one single moment.

The second simplest fact of life is that most people never rebound from what they perceive as a "fatal" mistake.

But it doesn't have to be that way.

There are ways to recover from seemingly fatal mistakes. This book details one such mistake I made and the techniques that I used to recover my life and to make a difference in my family's and my descendants' success.

At just eighteen years old, I ran away with the love of my life. I fled from Chicago, Illinois, to Cleveland, Ohio, against the advice of my mother, father, friends—even my enemies. I left my three-year-old son with my mom to pursue a career as a glamorous model. Turned out the man was a pimp, and my fellow models-to-be were prostitutes. I was slated to be the newest addition to the brothel.

We all make mistakes, and that was my own. Seemingly fatal, yes?

Instead, thirty years later, after having developed a series of techniques to change my thinking and deal with my bad decision head-on, I am now ready to comfortably retire as an Operations Vice President having worked at some of the top Fortune 50 companies in the US and UK.

Even now I recall how my past is a stark contrast from the life I achieved.

"I will never be a seven-dollar whore."

The words echoed in my mind as I sat back in the soft leather seat of a limousine. My driver, ever attentive, asked if I needed anything. I told him that I didn't as I sipped my smart water. I wasn't going to tell him we were riding past the very hotel where I had stood up to Baby.

I was in Cleveland to negotiate a new maintenance contract with our Japanese partners, a seventy-million-dollar deal. The driver had picked me up at the airport. He had a salad from Guarino's and ice-cold water waiting for me. I sipped my water slowly, picked at my salad, and thought again about Baby.

I remembered being in the lobby of the hotel. I was being trained as a "paid companion." That particular night I was assigned to observe the ladies as they went on their dates, collect the money when they came downstairs to prep for their next date, and then dispatch cleaners to the rooms to prepare them for the next encounter. All three ladies I was responsible for were having a busy night, so it was difficult to keep track of everything.

I had no idea if Prince, the pimp, was watching me or not. I had no idea, but I was on my toes in case he was. I was taking my instructions from Baby, who was in charge that night. I was dressed in a black suit, hair pinned up, beautifully sensible shoes, and a matching purse. Small diamond earrings accented my dark brown eyes. Baby came down and sat next to me. She informed me that I needed to come to the room with her.

"No," I told her. "I'm collecting the money."

Prince had not forced me to prostitute myself. . . yet. I was to dispatch and hold the money. If the ladies were arrested, any money on them would be confiscated.

Prince was busy with one of the other girls, so Baby discreetly grabbed my arm and squeezed. We didn't want to attract attention. "Tee, you will do what I tell you. I'm the one in charge."

Baby had successfully cowed me on many occasions, but not today. I continued to protest. "No, I'm not *your* whore."

Baby leaned in close to me. "You are whatever I say you are. You are my whore. You will do what I say. I'll charge what I want for you, tonight. A thousand, five hundred, fifty, or even seven." Baby laughed. "You'll be my seven-dollar whore."

I reached out and put my hand on Baby's arm and squeezed her hard. "I'm not your seven-dollar whore. I'm not the same girl who came here two months ago. I'm not that bitch. I'm the brand-new bitch you made me into. I will mess you up right here, right now, if you don't let me go. I'm not going upstairs."

We stared into each other's eyes.

"I will never be a seven-dollar whore. Never." I said it with such force that spittle came out of my mouth and landed on her cheek.

Baby wiped it off and let go of my arm. "I'm going to fuck you up," she said.

I laughed. "You are going to fuck me up more than I have fucked myself up?" I laughed again, bitterly. "That might be hard to do." I sat down and took a deep breath as she walked back to the elevator. Tears filled my eyes, but I didn't let them fall. This was all my own fault.

The car stopped moving, and I snapped out of my reminiscing. I thought about how blessed I was. I was respected in my company, one of the high-potential players. I had a decent career, a beautiful family, and a devoted husband who knew all about my wild years and did not care. In fact, he kept urging me to write a book about it.

As I walked into the skyscraper, I thought about how

strange it was to be back in Cleveland. What would I be doing now if I had not had the smarts to escape? Would I even be alive? I had been lucky in many ways. I had been very dumb in others. Perhaps my husband was right. When I had time, once the kids were grown, maybe I should write a book about my wild times.

This is that book.

People often lead poor lives because they cannot find a way out of their own self-made binds. They have no hope. They see no future. But I am here to say that there is always hope, always a possibility of a bright future. I have helped a number of people in desperate circumstances, especially women, change their thinking and find success despite their situations. I tell them my story and how I escaped my destiny.

I give myself as an example. No mistake or circumstance is escape proof.

There is no inescapable future.

An old Chinese proverb says, "A journey of a thousand miles begins with a single step."

Once you gain an understanding of how I escaped my fate, you will never be at the mercy of destiny again. You will be in control of your life. Your past mistakes will not define you or your future. You will identify and escape showstopper, life-changing decisions before becoming embroiled in them. You will kick existing bad decisions and/or habits to the curb. You will become so good at identifying and stopping these behaviors that I hope you will share this book, or even just portions of it, with others who need similar help.

Become the one who does good and spreads kindness to others by helping them make a second destiny for themselves.

Don't allow anyone to take your future away from you. No matter how mired in rottenness, or boredom, or plain bad activities you have become, your strength and power can take you out of that mindset and set you free. Set your future free.

Get out of the physical and mental mindset holding you back.

If doesn't matter where you are now—use my narrative to give yourself hope and make your life better. If I can do it, anyone can.

Once again: A journey of a thousand miles begins with a single step.

So, take that step, turn the page, and let us begin my story.

Chapter 2
Who Am I?

> "All good is hard. All evil is easy. Dying, losing, cheating, and mediocrity is easy. Stay away from easy." – Scott Alexander

I could've been a seven-dollar whore. Instead, I am retiring as a respected business professional after a successful thirty-five-year career. My last position was as the Vice President of Operations for a British aerospace company. In this chapter, we are going to discuss trust and trusting appearances too quickly.

I am a child of the Chicago projects. I grew up on the west side of Chicago, which was worse. My mother used to send us to the projects to get away from all the crime and ignorant things that were happening in the area where we lived. We would go to the projects to rest. My mom never graduated high school. My dad became a Chicago police officer because of a program that Chicago used to increase diversity in the police force.

They are not the reason I ended up in such a bad position.

I am the oldest of six children, and I'm older by about four years. There's me, the little princess, and then there are five stepchildren after me. My personality is a little bit conflicted. I was a princess for four years, and then I turned into the babysitter at my parents' demand and the default leader to five other children. That conflicted leader/follower mentality is one of the reasons I was able to get out of the bad situation that I was in.

Our family ended up moving to the south side of Chicago, which was even worse than the west side, but on the south side, my uncle had a house. My family moved in with my uncle and lived together in this one house.

I was a shy child, but smart. When I was fifteen, I was sent to a school specifically designed for pregnant teens. At this school, I was unwanted because I came from a highly technical high school and was in advanced placement classes. It was to my advantage to move through my classes as fast as I possibly could. There was no one else in the entire school that had advanced as far as I had in their education, so I had private classes with my teachers. The only class I took with the other girls was prenatal education. These teachers were not pleased to put together a lesson plan for only one student. Once I delivered my son that December, per my understanding, I was one of the few students allowed back into my original school to graduate. They sent me back to a regular high school and said, "No, uh-uh. She can't take up six teachers by herself." The bad girl turned back into a good girl because I was too smart.

My goal with this book is to help others who are trapped in dangerous situations recognize that there are ways to think that can be used as tools to escape and be free. You don't have to accept the destiny that was seemingly designed for you. You can make your destiny and define your future instead of going down the path that was chosen for you. You don't need to be what people perceive you to be but can be whatever you want to be. To do that, especially after you made bad mistakes, requires courage to overcome those mistakes. I hope my story can help you get out of a deep hole because in my lifetime I have gotten out of a number of hopeless situations.

Chapter 3
The Fatal Meeting

> "Only I can change my life. No one can do it for me." — Carol Burnett

The catalyst for the decision to run off somewhere, a disastrous decision, was that I felt helpless. I am now, and I was then, a voracious reader. I loved books, and one of the things I knew from books was that there was a different life out there—a glamorous life that wasn't tedious, boring, and sad. I worked at a doctor's that only paid five hundred dollars a month and had a commute of almost two hours one way.

I met Prince while waiting for my train. In Chicago, there are elevated stations that, when the tracks are clear, allow you to see the people on the other side. As I looked across the tracks, I saw the prettiest man I had ever seen. I thought, "Huh, that's a pretty guy." He looked across and saw me looking at him. He was dressed in blue jeans with a matching denim jacket, and his hair was tidy. He had gorgeous medium brown skin. Standing with him was a guy who was a little shorter with light skin, light eyes, and also beautiful. They waved at me, and I waved back.

They climbed down on the tracks to cross over to my side of the station, so they could talk to me, asking me who I was and what I was doing. Remember, I'm commuting for work, so I was in my all-white outfit with my little hat and pearl earrings— utterly different than what I really was: a project ghetto girl from the south side. I must have looked like a nurse angel.

They asked me what I did for work, and I told them I was a medical assistant headed home for the day. The man that I eventually ran off with, Prince, asked me for my phone number, but I declined. I told him I didn't give my phone number to men that I met at a train station, no matter how cute they were. He got on the train with me and rode about three stations before he got off.

For the next three days, he was there at the train station waiting for me. Each day I was resolved not to give him my phone number, explaining that I didn't know him from BooBoo the Fool. On the third day he won me over, and I finally relented. I gave him my number and told him he could call me and maybe we could set up a date.

Why did it work when he pressured me for my number on the third day? He told me that he was a photographer and was looking for new models. He told me he thought that I could be something special.

Specifically, he said, "I think you're something special because you're naturally highlighted. You have a beautiful profile around your eyes and your ears—the best I've ever seen. You have an excellent nose. You have all your teeth. When you smile you light up a room." I needed to hear that, so I gave in and resolved to give him a try.

He was picking up the wrong background from me because what he thought was that I was one of those nice lower-middle class girls that worked every day. He had no idea what my real background was, and that worked to my advantage in the end.

But there should have been some things I asked myself when he came to the station three times to talk to me, and one of those things would have been why a world-class photographer would need to find models in a Chicago train station. Ultimately, I didn't care at the time. I was flattered that Prince came to the train station three days in a row to get my number, and I wanted to hear that I was special.

But I ignored those red flags at that time. I didn't think it through and didn't pay any attention to the entire situation as much as I should have. I was dazzled by the handsome man in the beautiful clothes paying close attention to me at a time when I thought my life was boring, sad, and dull. I trusted the appearance of this man—the outward attractiveness was enough to sway my opinion. Everyone knows the saying about not judging a book by its cover. That saying goes both ways; don't assume something is bad because it looks terrible, and don't assume a man is good because he looks good.

I want you to do a simple exercise for me at this point. Watch a traffic light cycle through the colors. First, the light will be green, then yellow, then red. Only on stop is the light red on all four displays. The light is red on all four corners because it wants to hold all action, to allow nothing to go forward. When you meet someone new, I want you to hold on all four corners, until you have a clear signal to go. One of the tricks to getting out of a bad situation is not to get in it. I should've taken the time to ask more detailed questions and to find out what it was that Prince wanted from me before I jumped in with both feet. Next, we will take a look at how Prince swept me off my feet more than enough to continue to deteriorate my judgment.

Chapter 4
Come Into My Parlor, Said the Spider to the Fly

"Sometimes it's the smallest decisions that can change your life forever."—Keri Russell

Prince swept me off my feet. I should have paid more attention to the details of our growing relationship. There were warning signs that things would not go exactly the way I wanted.

Prince took me out a few times and discerned that I wanted to be a model. He told me he had experience in modeling and showed me pictures of three gorgeous women that he said he was representing. All I needed to do was follow his lead.

The first thing he did was change my look. Prince had tastes that were very different from my own. I admit that I liked tight clothing, but he loved short, tight, and expensive—especially expensive. He wanted me to look expensive in designer shoes, clothes, earrings. . . everything. It was the most expensive clothing I had ever worn in my life.

I was dazzled by all the beautiful things. These were all things I had wanted but couldn't afford before. I got to ride in nice cars, go to fancy parties where people were all dressed up and doing anything they wanted to do. That lifestyle was what I thought I wanted. I wanted what I thought everyone else had. He took the time to teach me how to do my hair and makeup, and then he took me around to different modeling agencies with professional headshots. I know now that you can't walk up to a modeling agency and get an appointment. Newcomers need to make an appointment. We had no appointments, so we got no appointments.

I believe that Prince planned those failed excursions purposefully. You must remember that I was not the corporate woman that I am now. Other than the unrealistic messages I received from my books, I knew nothing about appointments, modeling, or making it big. In the books, I read somebody was discovered when a stranger decided they were beautiful and BOOM—they're a multi-million-dollar model booking every cover and every show. But I believe Prince knew better. He knew that going to the different agencies and photographers without appointments would not get us anything. He knew we would not be seen. That was done on purpose to make sure I became discouraged in the Chicago modeling scene.

We must have gone to twenty or thirty places without getting a single call back. We did have one agency say that I had potential, but that was the most feedback we received. We didn't get anything other than that. Prince began to talk to me about Cleveland, where he was from. He said he had contacts and guaranteed I would be modeling with an agency and being paid within my second day there. I found out later that he was right. If I had wanted to model my second day in Cleveland, I could have been paid to do just that. But I did not.

Things were terrible at that time. I was very isolated. I wasn't working anymore and wasn't making time for anyone but my son. All my time was spent practicing my runway walk and making cold calls to try and be successful. But I was not successful at all. I was purposely isolated, so I only had one person giving input on my life. That input was from Prince.

And I was isolated. That was what Prince wanted of me. He wanted to make sure he was the only one telling me what to do. I resisted less and less over time. I didn't look like myself anymore. I didn't talk to anyone but him. He would say things he knew that I disagreed with, and I wouldn't bother to argue with him anymore. It was too much trouble. Prince was training me, preparing me for what it was that he wanted me to do.

I believe one of the things that protected me from ending up under Prince's total control was my aversion to drugs. When Prince offered them to me I simply refused. The reason I didn't do drugs was because of my mother. My mother refused to consume anything that had been handled by another person or that she could not confirm the source of. If one of her children tried to hand her pills, she would not even take those unless she had seen them specifically come out of the bottle and handed directly to her.

So, when Prince offered me some pills out of his hand and said, "Take these," I looked at them and thought to myself, *I'm not taking them pills*. But to avoid a fight, I took the pills, and I put them in my pocket. When he had marijuana, he licked the paper back and forth to roll up the joints and told me to smoke them. Everyone passed it around, and I pretended I was complying, but I never touched it to my lips. I didn't want their spit in my mouth.

When I had a drink at a club or restaurant, and I walked away from it, I didn't come back and continue to consume the same beverage. My mother trained me that if I didn't see the drink being poured if it was left unattended, or if I saw someone else touch it then I wasn't drinking it. So, I managed to escape the parties.

The second thing was that Prince loved these sexually expressive parties. He liked these crazy parties where there were a lot of strangers having sex. I had a fabulous technique for getting away from those parties because they never had enough of anything. As soon as the first piece of clothing came off, I would volunteer to refill something that had run out, and I didn't go back. They would have gotten so deep into what they were doing they wouldn't notice I was not there. So, I found a way to avoid participating in the drug-fueled craziness.

Once they took their drugs, no one knew who was there and who wasn't. So, it was effortless to slip out the back or go to a back room or sit in the car. My favorite—and you're going to laugh at this one—was to go into whatever room coats were stored in and slide under the bed and go to sleep. I would be woken up by the bustle when the people came in to grab their coats. As soon as the room was empty, I would slide out and pick up my coat. I would come out of the room like I had been at the party all the time. It wasn't a lie. I was there the whole time! In the bedroom, asleep under the bed. And it worked—Prince never caught on. I was pleased with myself for that small deception.

Prince also began to make suggestions of a relocation to Cleveland more frequently. Once we went to the train station to pick up a young woman, one of the models Prince claimed to be representing. I call her Baby because she had the biggest, brownest long-lashed eyes I'd ever seen. It was like looking at a baby's eyes. She also had a baby face with cute round cheeks and skin as dark as mahogany wood—a beautiful, stunning young woman.

Once Baby came into the picture things changed a bit. Baby's job, or so Prince said, was to make sure that I was to be prepared to be a model, so we could try to work with the agencies again. We would work to get me on the model track. I had some reservations about Baby's response when I asked where she had modeled. She gave me a strange look and told me that she had modeled at every level and had a lot of pictures taken of her but did not have any to show me. I found out later that she had not lied about having had a lot of photos taken of her.

The things that I should have noted as strange seem evident to me now. If Prince was representing these beautiful women, then where were the magazines, commercials, or print ads they were in? I saw the glamorous pictures, but no results. If Prince was a well-known producer, then why couldn't we get any meetings with anyone? Who was this third-party woman that showed up out of the blue? There is a lot of clarity when you look back on these kinds of things, but at the time I was so busy falling in love and being dazzled that I was oblivious to what seems obvious now. The devil is in the details, and the details of our love affair were skewed in his direction.

Prince's next move was to try to gain more control over me in yet another way. He had control of what I wore, what I ate, who I spoke to, and what I did with all of my free time, but he wanted control over my heart. There was another that I loved more than him—my son, Shawn. Luckily, I escaped that vicious move to capture my entire heart.

Chapter 5
Gangsta Daycare

> "It is hard to imagine a more stupid or more dangerous way of making decisions than by putting those decisions in the hands of people who pay no price for being wrong." –Thomas Sowell

Prince was making a play for full control of my body and soul. To do that he needed power over my son, and he almost got what he wanted.

I briefly wondered why Prince wanted me to put my child in what I have dubbed the "Gangsta Daycare." The arrangement I had with my mother was that she would watch my son for me while I went to work, I would pay her monthly phone bill, and we both got something out of the deal. Why did I call it "Gangsta Daycare"? First, it was in the Henry Horner projects. Second, the old woman running the daycare had "thug life" tattooed on her knuckles. Lastly, because although these children were little two-, three-, and four-year-old children, they looked like little gangsters.

How in the world could children that young look like they were up to no good? How could little kids be gangster? Their little faces were dirty. Their noses were running. They had on mismatched outfits. Not a single one of them looked happy. They all seemed old somehow. They looked sad. But they were well fed and were playing. To keep the peace with Prince, I put my son in that group. It was the cheapest daycare I'd ever had—five dollars a day, cash up front. You dropped your child off, and you would hand a five-dollar bill to the old woman. She would watch your child until you returned. Some kids seemed to stay all night, but not mine. I picked up my son every day at 5:30 p.m.

I signed my child up for this ghetto daycare, and I put him into it. He appeared to be okay with this arrangement for about two weeks. One day I came to pick up my polite and well-behaved three-year-old, and I couldn't tell him apart from the other children. He was dirty, nose running, wearing mismatched clothing that he had not had on that morning. He did not look happy. Another little boy had on his matching outfit. Wait. What? I walked in and confronted the lady about what had happened to my son, and her only response was that she didn't pay any attention to who had what clothes on. Sometime during the day my child had been undressed and redressed, and she had no idea when or why?

Because Prince was there, I calmly grabbed my son's hand and ushered him out with a promise of ice cream. I immediately made my way to public transportation and took it to 72nd and Stony Island. I walked into my mother's house and apologized fiercely, literally begging her to keep him for me again. Because that babysitting place was not a good environment for my child. That was not a good environment for any child. I truly believed that situation would have led to me having a child that lived a horrific life.

Of course, after I dropped Shawn off at my mother's house, I got right back on the bus and went back to the Henry Horner projects to where I had picked him up. When I walked back in without my son, Prince was not pleased. He questioned me about our agreement that Shawn would stay at this daycare. I was quick to think of a lie and explained that my mother had begged me to let him stay with her because she missed having him around.

For some reason, this upset Prince. He sat down on a couch and crossed his legs—staring at me.

"I asked you to keep the boy here," he said quietly.

In my naivety, I did not understand what he was saying to me. He was trying to tell me that I was violating some unspoken rule that existed. He was trying to imply that if he wanted it, that's the way it was going to be. Of course, that went straight over my head. I did not understand what the problem was. It was my child, and I took him to my mother's. Why was that a big deal? But it was a big deal to Prince.

Prince knew that after I removed my boy from this delinquent daycare that there was no longer any reason for me to come back to the Henry Horner projects. And my trips there became further apart. A quarter of my time was spent at my mom's house where my child was. Prince was always waiting for me when I picked Shawn up at the Henry Horner projects. Prince claimed to own a condo in downtown Chicago where I had visited him a few times. I know now that that was not his condo. I believe that he lived in the Henry Horner projects, and that condo was somehow borrowed on occasion. Prince had more control over me if my child was being taken care of in a place that guaranteed I would come to where he was every day.

I had been working as a medical assistant and making five hundred dollars a month. Because of Prince's influence, and because he individually scheduled "appointments" he knew would conflict with my work schedule, I was terminated from that job for an excessive amount of unexcused and unscheduled absences.

Once I didn't have a job, there was a new problem. Prince was sure that I was now broke, because as far as he knew all I had was the money in my wallet—sixty dollars. What Prince didn't know was that I had money being taken out of my paychecks and put into a savings account for emergencies. I wanted to make sure that I could always have a backup in case of an emergency and was able to stash close to a thousand dollars that he didn't know anything about. Baby showed up as soon as I was out of work to train me while I was considering going to Cleveland.

I think Baby showed up to handle me because I had told Prince some stories about my previous boyfriends. One of the things I told him was that I had only been hit once. Prince knew that it just took one time for a boyfriend to draw back and smack me across my face before everything he owned ended up on the curb in front of the house we stayed in. That was when I was seventeen. I put his stuff out there, and I left. I never saw that guy again.

I think one of the ways Prince controlled his women was to beat them. I was not down for hitting, and he knew he'd lose me if he tried because of the story I had told him. Besides, my dad was a Chicago cop. I was safe in Chicago.

The three of us ended up staying in a hotel, but I was in a room with Baby while Prince had his own room. Prince was supposed to be my boyfriend, so why was I sharing a room with Baby and not him? Again, what in the world was I thinking to ignore these signals?

I was too naive and silly to see that I was being naive and silly. I believed everything that Prince told me. I was not thinking or paying close enough attention. Remember what I said about contemplating and thinking? If I had merely taken a moment in my busy life to think, it could have given me insight to my behavior. Every day we were up and out doing unimportant things—just nonsense to stay busy. Going around and seeing people, and meeting people, and talking to people. None of that was real. Even though we went to some photography agencies and got some head shots done—we even went and spoke to other models about how they made it! That was the lie, that was not the truth.

Chapter 6
The Pledge

> "We are constantly faced with decisions. A lot of times, the right ones take more work; it takes longer to see benefit: they're the long route." – Tyler Joseph

I should have known better by this point, but I continued to ignore the signs. Prince's uncle came by to talk to Prince about what they claimed were investments they were planning. What happened was that they sat around smoking marijuana together.

After smoking a lot of marijuana, Prince turned to his uncle and said, "Let me show you something. Let me show you how much control I have over Baby." He told Baby, "Do the Prince pledge."

Baby stood up, put her hand over her heart, and started saying, "I pledge allegiance to Prince forever. He is ahead of me, my children, and everyone else. I will do everything I can to make sure that Prince's life is wonderful."

I was sitting on a couch thinking to myself, *What the hell was that? Baby, don't do that.* Then his uncle, with a mischievous smile, said, "What about this other one? Can you make this other one do it?"

I said nothing. Prince's uncle poked him again. I stood up to leave. I said, "I don't want to do the Prince pledge."

Prince stood up and said, "Come on Tee. Do the pledge."

As I walked out the door, I said, "I'm going to see you guys tomorrow."

I raced down the street to try and catch the bus. This is the problem with not having your own car. If I'd had a car, I would have gotten in it and driven away. But I didn't have a car, so I had to take public transportation.

As I was hastily making my way down the street, I look behind me to find that Baby was following. I was wondering why she was following me when she caught up and said, "Tee, you got to come back."

I responded, confused, "I'm not coming back. What are you talking about?"

"You got to come back. You got to come back now. You're going to be in a lot of trouble, and I'm not going to be able to save you." She sounded worried.

I said, "Baby, what are you saving me for? I'm not going to do this."

She grabbed my arm and started pulling me. We were two grown women getting ready to get into a fight on the concrete. I knew she was serious because she took off her heels and her jewelry. She was getting ready to beat me up to make me come back and say this stupid-ass pledge that I didn't want to say.

To deescalate the situation I said, "I'll go back with you, but I am not going to do it."

When she let go of me, I took off down the street like a nut, running as fast as I could to try and get away from her. Unfortunately, she was as fast as I was, and she caught up to me quickly.

She continued to beg, "Please, come back with me."

I finally relented and followed her back to the apartment. Prince looked at me and said, "Are you going to say the pledge?"

I responded, "I'm not saying any pledge. I'm not going to say the pledge. I'm not going to do a pledge to you, but I will promise to care for you and love you." His uncle was still smoking weed. He passed it to Prince and Baby, and they tried to give it to me, but no, I wouldn't take a puff.

So, he said, "You don't think there's anything I can do that'd make you say that pledge?"

"No," and I thought to myself, *Good job, Toni. Good job getting your baby boy out of here, because that would be the leverage he would use on you.*

But I was wrong. He went and got a coat hanger. He bent the coat hanger, and he looked at me, and he said, "You're not going to say the pledge?"

I said, "I am not going to say the pledge," and in response he took the coat hanger, and he whacked Baby as hard as he could across the back.

He said to me again, "You're not going to say the pledge?"

I responded, "I'm not going to say the pledge," and he hit her again with the coat hanger.

Baby and I were crying while his uncle laughed. Prince just stood there, solemn. "Are you going to say the pledge?"

I said again, "I'm not saying the pledge."

He went over to the stove and heated up the back of the coat hanger. When it was hot, he hit her with the hanger again, and again, and again. I finally said, "I'll say the damn pledge. I'll say the damn pledge. Stop hitting her."

As I stood there, he gave me the words to the stupid-ass pledge, and I said it. I said the stupid pledge filled with self-loathing and misery.

The thing that I thought was so crazy about this whole thing was that he knew not to hit me. But he knew that Baby was my teacher. Prince knew that hitting her with the hanger would eventually compel me to say the stupid pledge. And he was right.

What must I have been thinking to have stayed in a situation like that? I thought I was in too deep to back out now. No job, no friends—nothing.

I can also tell you that I had at least one time that I could have gotten away and gone back home with my mom. Baby, Prince, and I were out partying in an abandoned apartment building. There had to have been a hundred people there. Someone had cleaned out a floor of this abandoned building and put in gaming tables, there was a bar with free drinks, and every kind of bad person that you could think of was in attendance. It was a Mack party. For reference, in case you are unaware, *The Mack* was a black exploitation movie from 1973 about a pimp and his whores. They wore these fantastic, crazy clothes—fur coats and revealing sparkly dresses.

Everyone was dressed up like they were pimps and whores. There were drugs, alcohol, and money everywhere. Everyone looked wonderful, and they were laughing and having a really good time—until the police busted the place. We were not supposed to be in an abandoned building.

Now, the thing I find most interesting is I do believe many of those people were whores, pimps, and drug dealers. The police busted everybody and took them all downtown to search and fingerprint. This was one of those times where my decency saved me because they emptied my purse and didn't find what they expected to find. Among my effects was my work ID and my checkbook. There were no pills and no drugs in my purse. One of the older white policemen stopped and said, "Wait a minute. This one doesn't match. Don't fingerprint her. Looks to me like she's got a job."

Another policeman looked at me closely and said, "Isn't that Ben's daughter? Give him a call."

I didn't realize the kindness that the officer had shown me until much later in my life. If my fingerprints had gotten in the system, I would have had to explain that on every application for every engineering job I applied for later in life. Because the officers recognized me, in addition to not taking my fingerprints, they put me in my cell separate from everyone else. Everyone could see me when my father came in to pick me up. I was let out of the jail cell, handed my items, and walked away with my Dad—who was seriously pissed.

My reputation was ruined. My dad asked me, "What are you doing? What in the world are you doing? Are you doing drugs?"

I told my dad, "I'm not using drugs. I'm not doing anything wrong. I'm hanging out with these people, having fun. I want to be a model and these people are helping me do so."

He, of course, was disgusted. He dropped me off back at the Henry Horner projects and went about his business, but I'm confident that's one of the few times in my life that I disappointed my father terribly.

I didn't recognize how much I was being manipulated. If I had paid attention to what Prince was doing, and not what he was saying, I would have known that I needed to get away from him.

Chapter 7
The Fatal Mistake

> "Don't worry that children never listen to you; worry that they are always watching you." – Robert Fulghum

He was going to make me into a model and I was going to be as glamorous and beautiful as Baby—or so he said. I trusted him and believed every word he said, but I was not willing to gamble my child on him. Moving my child to my mother's was a great idea, because I would not have wanted Shawn to see Baby beaten or me forced to say that disgusting Prince pledge. But being embarrassed about the pledge was nothing compared to the body shots headed my way.

I apologized to Baby for the amount of time it took me to stop the beating by agreeing to say the pledge. She seemed to take the beating in stride saying that once we got back to Cleveland things would be much better for her. I should have listened carefully to her statement at that time. Things would be better for her, not us. They would not be better for me.

As Baby continued to show me more things that she wanted me to know, that Prince wanted me to know, I noticed the relationship between Prince and Baby. Perhaps the bond between them should have made me jealous. It turns out that Baby had known Prince since the sixth grade and had been with him all that time. Yet somehow she wasn't his girlfriend. I was. That was kind of a strange situation.

As we were trying to decide whether or not to go to Cleveland, I found myself needing somebody to talk to. I have five siblings, but they were teenagers—young and crazy like me—and everybody in our family was struggling to survive. They were trying to graduate high school and take care of themselves. They were trying to help the family as much as they could, so nobody was available to hear my indecision.

Talking to my mom would not have worked for me. Instead of graduating from high school, she had me when she was fifteen. She always wanted me to go to college because she thought I was book smart and not street smart. She would say that to me at least once a month. She would also say that I was weak, and she had no idea how I was going to make it. I already knew that a conversation with her would be either a horrible infinite circle or a dead end. Book smart, not street smart. Looking back, I think she was right.

I had a number of friends, but my friends did not like Prince. They didn't like the way I dressed or looked anymore. They didn't like how I had no time for anyone and couldn't go out or do anything. I never talked about books anymore. All I talked about was being a model and looking glamorous and wonderful all the time, and they didn't like that.

The only one of my friends who took the time to talk to me was Sharon. Sharon lived down the street from us. Her mom had died, and everyone knew that her dad and her brother were raping her, so no one wanted to play with her when she was small except for me. I was not allowed to go to her house, but she was allowed to come over to mine. We would play together, and we would hide while she cried under the covers in my bed.

I called her to meet for coffee and I told her about my plan to go to Cleveland. I said, "I'm thinking about going to Cleveland with Prince." She didn't say a word, so I let a couple of minutes pass, and I said again, "I'm thinking about going to Cleveland with Prince."

She looked at me and said, "You shouldn't go to Cleveland with Prince."

"What do you mean? He said he's got contacts there."

She said, "Prince is not a nice man and he does not care about you."

I responded, "Why would you say that, Sharon? Why would you say that about him?"

She explained, "The way he treats you is the way my father treated me. You're a trophy. You're something that he plans to use. The way he dresses you—you're like a doll. I wouldn't go to Cleveland with him, Tee. I wouldn't do it because it is not going to be good for you, and there's a lot of hidden things that I don't think you know about that man. You've only known him for four months and already you're going to go with him?"

I responded, defiantly, "Well, I think I'm going."

Sharon said something to me then that I think helped me and made my life easier once I fell into the trap. "Then don't take your child. Don't take your boy with you. You're going someplace you've never been before, you don't know anyone, and you're going to have a baby with you? A toddler? You don't want a toddler with you. You don't want a baby with you while you're trying to make it in the modeling world. What if they want you to model at 1:00 a.m. and you don't have anybody to babysit? How do you know what the conditions are down there in Cleveland? You don't know, so don't take your boy."

That advice I did take. When I left for Cleveland, my son stayed at my mom's house under her and my dad's protection. Leaving my son behind was the right decision.

I believed that if the people in Cleveland had the opportunity to see that I was special that I could be the best in the game. I wasn't the prettiest or the best walker, but I was the best package. I believed that. Part of it had to do with looking around at the magazines I'd seen. All of the girls looked the same, and even though I was not classically beautiful, I was striking. I could have changed the modeling business.

I hadn't even left for Cleveland yet before I recognized that I had perhaps not made the best decision. The very first hint should have been how we were traveling there. If I was running off to Cleveland with a big-shot photographer who was going to make me famous and put me on the covers of the glamorous magazines . . . why were we taking a Greyhound? There was something very wrong with that picture. The fact is that if something appears too good to be true, it usually is. There are no free lunches. Anything that an adult wants costs something. For me to believe that I would go to Cleveland and become a famous model with no dues to pay was outrageous, but I didn't recognize that then.

Chapter 8
Welcome to Tara

"Life is not always fair. Sometimes you get a splinter sliding down a rainbow." – Terri Guillemets

When we got off the bus in Cleveland, I could tell something was wrong. I could feel it. Prince's and Baby's attitudes were distinctly different. Suddenly, Baby and Prince were together, and I was the odd man out. When we stepped off the bus, Baby turned to me and smiled the brightest smile I had ever seen. Prince's brother was waiting for us to give us a ride to my new home.

When we pulled up to the house, I was stunned. I thought Prince was exaggerating about the house. I am certain the house exterior appeared in some movies. The house had a curved driveway with a very detailed iron gate covered with angels and devils grappling with each other. Prince activated the gate. The gate opened quietly—slowly and smoothly. There was a fountain in the middle of the drive, which was comfortably wide enough for two cars all the way around the fountain. Large-petaled flowers curled in a rainbow of colors around the fountain as clear, beautiful water flowed around a swirly pool. I got out of the car, walked over with my mouth open, and stuck my hand in the cold water of the fountain.

We went up the stairs, and Prince opened the door. The interior view was stunning. There was a large curved stairway, marble floor, and exquisite furniture. It was tastefully decorated. There were seven rooms downstairs and six bedrooms upstairs. Baby walked in and tossed her jacket on a chair. It missed and fell on the floor. She did not pick it up. Baby told me to follow her upstairs and I did. She walked me into a room with an unmade bed.

"This is your room."

I responded, taking in the room, "This looks as if someone is already living in here."

"Not anymore," Baby replied. "It's yours now."

The large room had a king-sized bed, small loveseat, fireplace, and two dressers. It had small roses on the coverlet. An oversized vanity mirror was positioned over one of the chests. A full-length mirror was behind the door. The carpet was gold, thick, and soft. I stepped over and opened a door that was draped in fabric matching the coverlet on the bed. Outside was a large patio with a small table and two chairs. Prince came up the stairs and told me he would give me a couple of days to get acclimated. Then we would talk. In the meantime, I was expected to do what Baby said. He went down the stairs and brought my luggage in before he left. I asked Baby where he went, and she told me he had gone home. It turned out Prince did not live at the same house I did. He had his own house somewhere else. This house was the most beautiful place I had ever been in, except that it was absolutely filthy.

There are times when you realize you've made a mistake that is going to be very tough to resolve. It only took two days in Cleveland for me to know it was going to be a tough situation to escape from. Day two was when Prince came into my room and closed the door. He sat on my bed and looked at me through heavily lidded eyes.

"So," he said. "Things have changed."

He then proceeded to slap me twice across the face, once in each direction. I was so astonished I didn't even feel any pain. Prince grabbed both of my shoulders and pushed me down on the bed, twisting my left arm behind my back. He whispered in my ear, "You belong to me. If you don't do what I tell you, I'm going to kill you. After I kill you, I'm going to hunt down your precious child and hurt him for years. You are going to do whatever I say, whenever I say." He twisted my arm even harder. "Do you understand? Nod your head, 'yes.'"

I nodded my head, and he let me go. I looked at him carefully, shielding my anger and rage. He watched me to see what I would do. I did nothing but look back at him. I said nothing. After a few minutes, he stood up and left.

Baby came into my room and sat on my bed. "You start work tomorrow. Your portion of the rent is a hundred dollars per day, cash only. Your first rent is due day after tomorrow, then every day after that. I'm going to take you over to your first modeling job. You can easily make a hundred dollars." Baby looked at me. "You should be scared of Prince."

I said nothing because I wasn't scared. I was furious.

But my first modeling job! I was excited. After that special talk with Prince, I should have known better.

Chapter 9
The Ladies

> "He saw the darkness in her beauty; she saw the beauty in his darkness." –Several Citations

All of Prince's women were striking. Some were beautiful in the traditional way, while others simply grabbed your attention and you couldn't take your eyes off of them. It took me about a month to learn each of their stories.

Baby was the "bottom bitch." Her job was to manage the rest of us to ensure we produced money and followed orders. She also got to spend more time than anyone else at Prince's house. I hadn't been allowed in the master's house because I was not adequately trained. I was not producing what I should have been as a trainee whore because I was not whoring yet. Baby met Prince in the sixth grade where he immediately began taking advantage of her. Her mother made her lunch each day before school. Prince had no lunch, so she gave him hers. This meant that Baby often went without lunch, because most of the time he would not share her lunch with her.

Baby had a criminal record because of Prince. They were stopped for a traffic violation. There were two pounds of marijuana in a backpack in the truck. Baby told the police that it was her backpack and Prince had nothing to do with it. She went to jail to cover for him. She could make you believe that she was on your side, that she was your friend, but she was Prince's girl through and through.

Baby was not worried that I would escape my fate. She believed that I still loved Prince as much as she did. If Baby had a choice between herself and Prince, Prince would win every time. If I had a choice between Prince and me, it was me every time.

Essence was Prince's number two, but she wanted Baby's top spot more than anything. She was the most beautiful of us all. She had once toured with the Essence fashion show as their top model. She was in magazines, on television, and a spokesmodel for the magazine. Tall, slender, and fine boned. She had large natural breasts, a slim waist, and flowing hips. Her eyes were light brown—so light they sometimes looked clear. She was also biracial, which meant she had bronze highlights that appeared naturally in her hair, which she added more highlights. Her hair sparkled when she walked in the sun.

Essence met Prince at an exclusive after party for an Essence fashion show. She was already hooked on cocaine and was hurting for a fix. Prince recognized the symptoms, walked over to her, showed her a package of snow in the palm of his hand, and she followed him out of the room and into prostitution. She never went back. She said that the fashion showrunners had finally figured out why she was missing so many appointments, so her remaining time was limited anyway. I don't know that I believed that, but it's the story I was told.

The way Baby told the story was that Essence stayed in a drug haze for six weeks because Prince was supplying her with drugs. During that time, Prince turned Essence into a full-blown prostitute. Prince did not worry about controlling her, even when she had managed to cut her habit down from two hundred dollars a day to only twenty-five dollars a day. They had another lever that kept her turning expensive tricks. Essence was an escort before those kinds of services were common.

She met her clients at the expensive hotel, and she showed up looking classy. They had dinner, drinks, and pleasant conversation. Essence had two years of college credits under her belt and read newspapers daily, so she was a good conversationalist. Her political views and interests matched whomever she was with. How surprised would those high-paying clients have been to realize that when Essence was not with them, she was a low-end, one-hundred-dollar whore?

Essence wanted Baby's job. It was no secret she wanted to be the bottom bitch. Because of this well-known desire, Baby punished her. If there was a nasty or unusual request from a customer, Baby routed it to Essence. If Baby thought this was deterring Essence, she was wrong. The lousy treatment only made Essence want the upgrade even more.

The thing Baby did not understand was that Essence was

an incest victim. She didn't care what happened to her body. She escaped to another place in her mind no matter what was going on with her body. Essence was not there during the humiliating and hurtful experiences Baby set up as punishment.

Essence grew up in a very small town in Mississippi with a population of less than a thousand people. Essence was a beautiful little girl. Her mother left her abusive husband when Essence was only four, leaving Essence behind. He married again before Essence turned five. He started molesting his daughter when she was ten—taking her virginity. Her uncle joined in when she was eleven. Her second uncle a few months later. Eventually, all three of them were taking turns repeatedly doing unspeakable things to her. This went on until she was fifteen when someone contacted her birth mother, Sage. Sage returned, armed and pissed off. Essence left with her mom that same day.

Irish was the girl who arrived at the house a few weeks before me. She hailed from a small village in Ireland. Natural red hair, red eyelashes, pale white with freckles, green eyes, and the best smile. She was not slender, but she was strong. She gave off a natural exuberance that grabbed your attention and held it. When she was in the room, she gave you the feeling that everything was going to be alright. Her special something came from the inside, clawing its way out and putting an unseen glow around her. When she walked into the room, all eyes were on her. I don't know how she met Prince, because she wasn't there for Prince. She was deeply in love with Baby, so she was whoring for her. Baby met Irish at a spin class and an intense love affair followed soon after. Eventually, Irish was working for Prince to stay close to Baby. How Baby manipulated her into that position I do not know, but every penny she made went into Prince's pocket.

Irish's room was right next to mine. I heard her sobbing hopelessly every night, talking to herself and praying to her Catholic God. Each night I heard her pray for the strength to leave Baby. Each evening she went with the other girls when Prince came to pick them up.

I was the newest money-making whore, or so Prince hoped. The image Prince and Baby had of me was wrong. Their view of me was of a gentle lower-middle class medical assistant that they could eventually bend to their will. They were sure I was going to be a very productive whore once I was trained.

Prince and Baby had no idea that my cousin and I had taken baseball bats with us to defend ourselves as we climbed up the stairs in the projects when the elevator was out. They had no idea that drug addicts were an everyday part of my childhood. You stepped over them if they blocked your way and watched where you played to avoid needles. I fought a lot of fights with other kids. I had defended myself from a number of rapes. They had no idea that my grandfather was a grifter who made his money cheating people and running cons. They didn't know that my decision to leave my son with my parents, instead of bringing him to Cleveland, was because some part of me knew Prince was too good to be true.

Prince did not live with us but had his own place about ten minutes away. Every night someone got to go home with Prince. Baby went most nights, but sometimes he chose the biggest money maker or scammer of the night. I had not been picked since arriving at Tara. No Prince time was part of my punishment for not being a whore.

Chapter 10
Filth Buys Me Time

> "You just do it. You force yourself to get up. You force yourself to put one foot before the other, and God damn it, you refuse to let it get to you.
> You fight. You cry. You curse.
> Then you go about the business of living. That's how I've done it. There's no other way. "
> —Elizabeth Taylor

The house was perfect except for the fact that it was disgusting. Dishes piled up in the sink, dust everywhere, and clothes were strewn all over the house. When the girls came back from tricking, they would take off their panties and put them in a basket in the bathroom. I found out that instead of washing the panties, they would simply buy more.

I was afraid and anxious about my future, knowing I had made a terrible mistake. When I need to think, I eat. When I need to plan, I cook. Eating soothes me and being in motion helps me think. There was no food in the refrigerator and everything needed to be cleaned, so this was an ideal situation for me to think up a plan. It took quite a while to clean everything up and get a meal cooked for the other girls and me. This gave me a lot of time to think and plan.

An added benefit to my need to keep moving was that it improved things for the other girls. Not having to run out and buy something to eat gave them more time to leave without having to rush around. Eventually, I was going out with the girls. Prince said I needed to go out with the girls and watch them work. I recorded how many tricks I saw them turn in a little book Prince assigned to me. This is how my training began.

Irish ran away while Prince and Baby were attempting to get me trained. Irish slipped out because they were both busy keeping an eye on me. It took them three days to find her. I don't know how she was punished, but she was back turning tricks after two days of rest.

The night Irish was back at work I had gotten dressed to go out for my training. Baby met me at the bottom of the stairs to tell me I could stay home until Irish was trustworthy again. Prince and Baby didn't have the time to keep an eye on me while they couldn't trust Irish to remain where she was expected to be.

This turn of events worked in my favor. Maybe Baby and Prince didn't see it, but I watched Irish in the quiet moments. She had not learned any lessons and was just biding her time while she waited for her next chance to escape. My goal was to keep my head down while I plotted and planned my own escape. I'd comply with their demands, but I still had a few tricks up my sleeve. I was going to concentrate on what I could do to exploit any opportunities that came my way. I learned a lot as the oldest child of so many kids, and I knew those skills had saved my skin more than once. I was going to use whatever skills that could help me to get out of this hell.

Everyone must work with what they have. Use what you've got to get what you need.

A few weeks after we arrived at Tara, Prince told us he was inviting his mother over for dinner. He wanted her to meet his new girls. She was a nondescript older woman, educated and soft-spoken. You had to lean in to hear what she was saying. I made lamb chops and cornbread and served it with grape Kool-Aid. We had store-bought chocolate cake for dessert. It felt like a typical family meal, and I almost expected us to start singing Kumbaya while we held hands and swayed from side to side.

The thing that startled me most about this interaction was when Prince left the room. He was gone for only a moment, but his mother took that opportunity to lean over to me and tell me to get out. She told me to go home as fast as my legs would carry me. She had seen what had become of the nice girls that got involved with her son and she thought it better that I be on my way.

When Prince returned, carrying the chocolate cake, his mother resumed her calm expression and began commenting on how nice the house looked.

Chapter 11
Be a Model

> "You have brains in your head. You have feet in your shoes. You can steer yourself any direction you choose. You're on your own. And you know what you know. And YOU are the one who'll decide where to go…" —Dr. Seuss

On my third day, the day after Prince hit me, Baby and I jumped into her red Mustang and headed toward downtown Cleveland. We stopped at a building on the edge of downtown that looked as if it had seen better days. When we walked in, we were hit in the face with some of the most obnoxious smells. It smelled like a musty old man—like cigars mixed with stale aftershave, with hints of onions and chili. We went up the elevator and got off on the fifth floor. I noticed candles and cherubs everywhere.

Baby walked me into an office where a receptionist sneered at both of us as she waved her hand toward the back before buzzing us through. A man with a high forehead and protruding eyes sat behind a desk. He smiled a nasty smile at me. "Another one from Prince?"

Frog Eyes handed me a clipboard with a few forms and instructed me to fill it out. The clipboard held a blank job application, a W-4 form, and a model release form. I dutifully filled all of them out while Baby and Frog Eyes kept a close eye on me. Frog checked in with me occasionally to make sure I understood all of the forms, which I did.

Once I completed the paperwork, he asked for my driver's license, which he made a copy of before returning it to me. All the while Baby was watching me carefully. She told him I could start tomorrow. He came from behind the desk and said, "Come on, I'll show you around. Tomorrow you can tell me what level you want to start at."

As we walked out, I recognized one of the girls from Tara. Irish was sitting on a chair wearing nothing but her panties. When she saw Baby, she jumped up and smiled broadly. This was when I figured out that Irish was in the game for *Baby* . . . not Prince.

Frog Eyes was telling me to read the request slips as they came in and to dress for the appropriate customer. He pointed to a massive collection of clothing. He told me I would get twenty-five dollars for the best customers. We walked out into a large area that had floor to ceiling cubicles. Frog Eyes stopped and opened a little window in the back wall, and I got a glimpse of a young woman in a skimpy sailor costume with a fake smile and posing for a fat man with a camera. I was very confused by what was happening. I found out later that this particular posing paid ten dollars per customer.

Behind a different set of walls were similar photo sessions taking place, only these women were topless. Frog Eyes informed me that we got fifteen dollars per customer for those kinds of sessions. Finally, he stopped in front of the last two cubicles.

The women were completely naked. These were the twenty-five dollar per customer sessions. Baby told him I would be there the next day.

After we walked out the door, I told Baby I was not going back because that was *not* the type of modeling I wanted to do. She told me she didn't give a shit and that I would have to do it. When I got home the next night, I had to have her hundred dollars or there would be hell to pay. She was ugly about it—her face twisted and angry. Not exactly a good look for her.

The next morning, I was up and out early. My goal was to find the nursing and geriatric homes in the area. I knew that all nursing homes were habitually short on staff. I rang the bell at the first place I identified. When the door was answered, I asked for the laboratory manager. At the third nursing home, I hit payday. For fifty bucks—cash—I would collect all of the specimens due each day. Blood, urine, and feces. It is especially difficult to draw blood from many older adults. It is horrific to work with sleepy older people to collect specimens, but I was very good at getting older people to cooperate with me. I was done at the nursing home by 6 a.m. They paid me from petty cash and replenished it each day. It was like I was never there. The patient specimens simply appeared in the labs each morning neatly labeled before the technicians arrived.

After the nursing home each morning, I went to get day

work. I stood in line for factory assembler jobs. They drove us to the factories and picked us up at the end of the workday. This provided me with one hundred and four dollars per day. A hundred bucks for Baby and four left over for me. I also kept an extra two hundred on me from my emergency bank account in case of a bad day. It didn't matter to Baby where I got the money each day, as long as I got it to her by the end of the day.

Baby was the overseer. I knew this game, and I knew Baby and Prince would merely move my target up higher until I had no choice but to participate in nude modeling. Nude modeling was the gateway drug of whoring. My thoughts and opinions had no value. What I wanted to do no longer mattered. I was a money machine to be exploited to the maximum. I needed to find a way to become valuable, but not to sell my soul to do it. Having a small amount of savings in the bank made a difference. I had found a way to survive, for now, but it was grueling.

Prince and Baby had a set a trap for me that appeared inescapable. I was like a bear with my leg caught in the snare. I was no longer in love with Prince if I ever had been. He had made a believable threat to my child and me. Baby's job was to control my physical presence. This trap had worked so many times and on so many women. What they did not count on was my ability to subvert a situation once I saw its potential. They weren't prepared for this bad bitch.

Chapter 12
How Deep Is Your Love?

> "All warfare is based on deception. Hence when we are able to attack, we must seem unable; when using our forces, we must seem inactive; when we are near, we must make the enemy believe that we are far away; when far away, we must make him believe that we are near." –Sun Tzu

I had been in the house about a month when I decided to tell Essence what I figured out the first time I saw her. I woke her up much earlier than the other girls and asked her to go for a walk with me. In a resigned manner, she followed saying, "You want me to tell you all about the fast life?"

"No," I said.

"What then?"

I took a long breath. "Your eyes are very unusual, but I have seen eyes exactly like that before."

Essence froze and looked at me. After a moment she said, "What? You have seen eyes like mine before? Where?"

"On a small boy, in Chicago," I said. "I have a son. He is almost three years old. Prince had me put him with a new babysitter. There was a four- or five-year-old boy with your eyes."

She took a breath. I had no idea that she was holding her breath. "Marco." Tears started pouring down her face as she repeated his name, "Marco."

There was a bench nearby, so we sat down. She cried—sobbed—for a long time before she spoke again. "Prince took Marco away from me seven months ago because I wanted to leave the business. I found a job as a greeting hostess. It wasn't much, but it was enough to pay the rent of a cheap place I found. Since then, I get photos of my little boy every week. I didn't know he wasn't in Cleveland. Prince didn't go to visit his brother in Chicago; he took Marco out of my reach."

I looked at her sternly and said, "You can't tell Prince what I told you. He would lose his mind."

She smiled at me. A sad, wry smile. "No. I won't tell. He won't know that I know where Marco is. He told me he would find me and hurt Marco if I ever ran away. Thank you for telling me. Why did you do it?" Her eyes narrowed. As the initial shock wore off, she became suspicious of my intentions. "What do you want?"

I looked back at her calmly and reassuringly said, "I couldn't stand the idea of you not knowing where your child was. I'm a mother, too. Let's go back. You need to wash your face and get back in the bed so that this meeting never happened. "

Essence smiled at me. "I owe you a big favor now. You won't be sorry you told me about my son."

"Essence," I said. "You don't owe me anything. I hope you would have done the same for me."

She smiled that wry smile again. "Maybe." She paused. "Maybe not. That is why you are lucky to have made me your friend."

Essence didn't know it, but my helping her with no expectation of quid pro quo made me feel like a decent person. That feeling of basic human decency was priceless. It was a feeling I seldom had access to at Tara.

My days were filled with the same routine I established at the beginning of my stay at Tara. I worked the nursing home in the morning collecting specimens, then stood in line for the assembly jobs at the factory. I worked long hours, and I was exhausted. But I wasn't whoring, so I felt like I couldn't complain too much. Besides, I didn't have anyone to complain to.

About a week after my conversation with Essence, I knew something was up. I could feel it, but I couldn't quite put my finger on it. I had been at the house for five weeks. I got home from work to find Baby waiting for me. She told me I needed to get dressed and informed me that I was going out with Prince alone that night. I didn't like that idea. I had managed to avoid being physically intimate with Prince since I came to Cleveland. My feelings were very confused, and intimacy was not going to add clarity. I didn't want to go out on a date with him. I didn't want to see him. I was turning in my one hundred dollars a day. I was working my ass off, but I had not yet figured out how to get out of that place.

That morning, Essence snuck into my room very early. She whispered in my ear, "Tonight is the night. Don't believe anything." She pressed something into my hand. "You will know when to use this. Hold it until the right moment. Tell Prince you won the lottery today. Make sure you know the winning numbers. Tell him it was going to be a surprise." The thing in my hand was a wad of money. I was stunned. Where had Essence gotten the money and why was she giving it to me?

I did what I was told. I showered and put on the dress and shoes Baby gave me to wear. She fixed my hair and did my makeup before handing me a matching purse. I managed to stuff my lipstick and the six hundred bucks Essence had given me into the little purse. I was waiting outside when Prince pulled up to retrieve me. I got in the car and he said, "Tee, you look great. We're going to go to a party at a friend of mine's tonight." I thought that was strange because usually Baby went to the private parties.

It was a good party. There were musicians on stage that I recognized. TV show personalities were engaged in casual conversation. Everyone seemed to be having a lot of fun. I relaxed and started trying to enjoy myself. I made conversation and was enjoying feeling normal again, even if it was probably only going to be for a little while. Maybe this was only a party. Maybe there really was no whoring involved.

Prince ruined that illusion quickly as he approached me

with a sturdy looking gentleman by his side. The gentleman was white, but with attractive dark features. At over six feet tall, and I would guess about two hundred and fifty pounds, it seemed odd that he had bodyguards with him. He looked across the table at Prince and said, "This is her?"

"Yes. This is her." Then Prince turned to me and said, "Hey, I need you to do me a favor."

I looked at him suspiciously and responded with, "Oh, a favor?"

He said, "Yeah. I left my wallet at home, so I don't have any money on me. I owe Ed here five hundred dollars. Ed said if I don't give him his five hundred dollars right now, he's going to have his two guys take me out in the bush and beat the living shit out of me until they get five hundred dollars' worth."

I was stunned. Even though Essence had told me something was coming, I was still stunned by what Prince was trying to do to me. My grandfather had called this one the "You a Sucker" scam. It worked well as long as the sucker thought they were saving a loved one from a horrible fate. The fraud took many forms, and Prince was playing his version out pretty well. I guessed he had run this scam a hundred times.

I innocently asked, "What does this have to do with me, Prince?" I knew my mark.

"Well, Ed thinks you are one sexy woman. He said that if you would give him a blowjob, he'll write off the entire five hundred dollars. There's a bedroom upstairs. You and he can go up there discreetly. Once you give him a blowjob, he will forgive the entire five hundred dollars."

I said, "Prince, I want to make sure I understand. You owe him five hundred dollars?"

"Yes, I owe him five hundred dollars," Prince said.

"You don't have the five hundred dollars with you?" I asked.

"No," Prince said.

"But I'm certain we have five hundred dollars back at Tara, back at the house," I responded sweetly.

Prince didn't miss a beat and said, "Yes, but Ed is not willing to wait for it. He wants his money right now. So, you have to give him a blowjob right now."

Prince looked deep into my eyes and he said, "How much do you love me? How deep is your love? Are you willing to see me beat to crap over a single, lousy blowjob?"

I winced, thinking about how ashamed I was to be in this situation. My grandfather would spin in his grave. Prince took my wince to mean he had gotten to me—that he was winning this game. He pressed on. "How much do you care about me? If you cared for me, you would do this for me."

I stared at the floor. I could feel any love I had left for him sliding out of my feet and out onto the floor like a living thing. I was a mark, nothing more. I was a *sucker* to this man. Prince thought he had me. His voice was soft and sweet. "Tee, you would make sure I don't get hurt. You would be my girl. You would be my savior. It's one lousy blowjob."

I said, "Yes, you're right. How much money do we owe him again? I want to make sure I understand." He confirmed the debt was five hundred dollars, and then he smiled that beautiful hundred-watt smile at me, knowing I was going to acquiesce. I stood up at the same time that Ed did, and he reached for my hand. I did not take his hand. Instead, I reached into my purse. I pulled out the money I had stuffed in with my lipstick earlier. I had six hundred dollars. I counted out five hundred dollars for Ed, and I handed it to him. I looked at Prince and said, "There is nothing I wouldn't do for you, baby. I think we have a much better solution."

At that moment, I knew that I was one blessed woman. I had struggled with telling Essence where her little boy was. I was so worried about the consequences if Prince or Baby had found out. But I was all in. My heart told me that I needed to tell Essence, and so I did. Her heads-up regarding this situation had prepared me for something unusual. Her money had helped me escape this time.

When you talk about changing your destiny, being a decent person counts. The kindness that I showed another person with no expectation of anything in return saved me from becoming a whore that night. The rule in this situation was simple: once you performed a sexual act for money, you have turned into a prostitute.

My grandfather once told a joke about a man who saw a beautiful young woman and asked her a simple question. "Would you have sex with me for a hundred dollars?" According to the story, she resisted, but the man persisted. "Would you have sex with me for two million dollars?" This time she agreed that two million dollars was enough to convince her to have sex with the man, so he continued,

"Will you have sex with me for two hundred dollars?" She resisted again, her reasoning being that she had already turned down the one-hundred-dollar offer, but the man continued, "Well you said you'd do it for two million dollars, so all we're doing is negotiating price."

What Prince had been trying to do was make me into a whore. If I had given Ed a blowjob for five hundred, I would have been his whore.

Prince never asked me where I got the money from. I think he didn't want to know the answer.

Chapter 13
God Don't Like Ugly

"Sometimes by losing a battle you find a new way to win the war." –Donald Trump

I found my way out of a compromising situation because I chose to be a good person to someone I expected nothing from in return. This was one of the reasons I managed to walk away from the situation with Prince and his friend, Ed, without having to compromise myself further. Essence, while unable to provide specific details about the situation I was heading into, did manage to give me a warning and the stash of money to help me escape. I had pondered what I would do if asked to prostitute myself for Prince. How could I refuse and what would be the consequences if I failed to comply? What Prince was counting on in that situation with Ed was the element of surprise and a lack of funds.

The urgency of my situation was driven home to me that night. The second attempt to convert me into a sexual cash cow for Prince had failed, and that wasn't going to make him happy. Until I turned that first trick, I was not his whore—I would never be *his* whore. I had no intention of turning that trick. I vowed I would never compromise myself completely. Not for Prince, or Baby, or anyone else. I had begun to figure out the rules to this game I was playing.

Irish ran away a second time six weeks later, with both Prince and Baby keeping an eye on her. This was a stunning development. It took Prince and Baby six days to catch her and bring her back that time. When she returned, there was a different Irish in her place. She was a zombie. Whatever they had done to her had created a new problem. No man wanted to pay top price to make love to a zombie. So, my training was delayed, once again. I was beginning to learn what the whore career path was, and it was not pretty.

There was another group of whores working for Prince. I thought that Prince went home each day after he dropped off the ladies, but soon after Irish's second escape attempt, I learned where he went every night. He went to manage his streetwalkers.

Streetwalkers worked all the time with only small breaks in between. These whores were drug-addicted women who got between ten to fifty bucks per trick. They walked the streets taking on men on their lunch hour, unemployed men, or even homeless men. Anyone who could pay the price of admission, and it didn't matter how they looked or smelled. These girls gave Prince all of their money. In return, he provided protection and drugs for them. He got them out of jail when they were picked up. He offered a place for them to sleep and eat. Most of them were arrested pretty often.

I learned about the streetwalkers the day Baby woke me up early before the rest of the ladies came in. She told me to get dressed because I had an errand to run with Prince. I got dressed and went downstairs just as Prince was dropping off the other ladies. Without a word, I climbed into the passenger seat.

He was completely silent as we rode toward the middle of town. After about twenty minutes he pulled over. A tall, heavy-set pregnant woman got in the back seat. She handed Prince a wad of money. "Daddy," she said. "One of my best nights."

"This is Diamond," Prince said, introducing her. "You'll be with her today. She needs to go to the prenatal clinic at the downtown Planned Parenthood."

Diamond protested loudly, "Daddy I told you I could do it alone! This is my third baby. I know what to do. I don't need no clinic. I don't need this girl with me after she been working all night."

Prince replied, "This is a virgin, she ain't been out yet." Then he turned to me and said, "Diamond is very good at giving people the slip, so she won't have to see the doctor. I'm holding you responsible for making sure she sees the doctor today. You understand?"

I nodded and said, "I understand."

Prince dropped us off at the Planned Parenthood. It was a nondescript medical building in the middle of a stretch of nondescript medical buildings. Prince handed me a wad of cash to pay for the appointment and drove off.

Diamond was smiling and waving as Prince drove away.

The moment he was out of sight, a different Diamond emerged. She grimaced and bent over slightly at the waist. Diamond looked as if she was in a lot of pain.

"I need a fix right now before we go to the clinic. Right now." She was persistent and demanded the money Prince had given me.

I looked at her sternly and said, "No."

"We can do this the hard way or the easy way." She said, demanding the money again.

I looked at her with astonishment. I needed to talk to her in her language. I told her, "Bitch, no. I'm not going to give you a single dollar until you go to the clinic. What kind of fool do you think I am? If I give you any money, I won't see you again and my ass will be in trouble. Come over here to try to take the money from me and I'm going to kick you in the stomach."

She told me that if I didn't give the money to her, she was going to "whoop my ass." I looked at her and said, "Then that is an ass whopping I am going to have to take because I am not giving you this money." Diamond looked startled, stood still for a moment, straightened up, and started laughing. "Come on, Virgin. Let's go to the clinic so we can get something to eat." She laughed heartily as we walked in. She was not in pain. It was all a ruse. I found none of this funny.

When we signed in at the desk, the receptionist sneered at me. "Is this yet another one of your sisters accompanying you to the clinic, Christine?"

Christine laughed, "This here is Virgin."

The receptionist handed Christine a form to fill out, so I could receive her medical information and be in the room with her when the doctor examined her. We completed the preliminaries and sat down in the waiting room to wait for the doctor. She asked me if I was living in the big house. When I responded in the affirmative, she began to open up to me.

"I used to live there," she said. "I lasted four years before I had to walk the street. Baby makes sure everyone moves down eventually. Drugs got me. I'm a stone-cold addict now. I was shooting, sniffing, eating, or smoking whatever I could get off the tricks. I couldn't continue high-class escorting when I was high every chance I got." She laughed. "That was a pun. With these tracks on my arms, I've got to street walk. At first, I shot between my toes . . ." She trailed off for a moment, just long enough for me to think about what she had said. I thought to myself, *Holy shit. Is this where I'm headed?* My face must have reflected my thoughts because Diamond grimaced at me.

"You worried you going to end up like me? I'm worried I'm going to end up in the van, girl. This ain't the lowest. Ask Baby about the van."

The medical assistant called Christine's name. We saw the doctor with no further discussion. He checked Christine, told her everything was fine, then wrote prescriptions for prenatal vitamins and allergy medication. I filled them for her at the on-site pharmacy. Christine was doing well, and the doctor was pleased she showed up for her appointment, but he was not pleased she was still shooting dope. He spoke to her about the torture that the baby would undergo once born. She told him she had cut her habit by fifty percent, but she couldn't stop. Once delivered, the baby was going straight into the detox at St. Joe's Hospital and would never see its mother again.

I called Prince from the pay phone to let him know we were done with the appointment. He showed up twenty minutes later to pick us up. I got in the back seat. Christine rode up front. Prince handed her a small cellophane package. She took the bag and looked back at me. "You want some of this?" she asked.

"Nope," I said. "All for you."

Christine leaned back and smiled. "I wasn't giving you none anyway, Virgin."

It was a few days later before I had the chance to talk to Baby alone. I asked her what Christine meant about the van. Baby laughed hardily. "You don't need to worry about the van. You'll never work there."

I insisted on knowing what the van was and why Christine was so terrified of it. After some persistence, Baby finally told me that Prince would run specials for working men as a punishment for streetwalkers who committed an egregious crime, such as stealing from him or running away. He would put the girl in a rented van with a mattress. He would drive it to his old neighborhood and park it in a dingy alley. There, in the dirty, garbage-strewn alley, he would run a special all day.

Ten bucks a pop. The van was the punishment Irish received that broke her will after she ran away the second time. Prince put Irish in the van for a day. Not for the usual ten dollars a trick, but for seven. Holy shit. Knowing that it was no wonder to me that she was in a dark place. And now I knew where Baby got her "You'll be my seven-dollar whore" speech from.

The second thing I wanted to check was the insinuation Christine made about no one staying at the house long-term except for Baby, but I didn't ask. Baby had known Prince for almost sixteen years. Essence had been in Tara for three years, and Irish arrived right before I did. Where were all the women that had come before us? The only consistent one was Baby. I suspected that Christine was right. No one but Baby would be with Prince long-term. Everyone else would eventually be in the van.

The discussion that I had with Baby about the van was the straw that broke the camel's back, as they say. Since I wasn't a producer, I was never in his bed. Since I wasn't hoeing, Prince would barely talk to me. Irish's shenanigans were occupying all of his thoughts, so I had become invisible since the night with Ed and the five hundred dollars. I knew that one day Irish would straighten up and fly right, and on that day I would be visible again. I was changing, and not for the better. The craziness was starting to look normal to me. I had to get out of there.

Chapter 14
I'm Not That Bitch Anymore

"Pay no attention to the man behind the curtain."
L. Frank Baum, *The Wonderful Wizard of OZ*

In the four months I was at Tara, there were only two major altercations. It was good that both took place toward the end of my stay. One was my rebellion at the hotel; the other was over a pair of shoes. I had seen and heard so much nonsense that I was deep in the crazy with them. Crazy things were starting to seem fine to me.

Someone had taken my white nursing shoes out of my room. I needed the shoes to go to work. I asked everyone except Baby, because she was asleep. No one had any idea where my shoes were. Unfortunately, that meant I had to wake up Baby. Baby did not like her sleep disturbed. She outright told me she took my shoes since she had decided it was time to stop the nonsense. I needed to get out and make some real money. I reminded her that she already had a trainee—Irish. I had learned that Baby was taking on extra tricks to make Irish's money so that Irish did not attract Prince's attention. Apparently, Irish had been crying after every trick, and that was not good for business. Baby had *not* told Prince of these new developments. She was trying to bring Irish around, so she could start earning the good money on her own. Irish needed to be independent enough to not require babysitting.

I closed her bedroom door so that we could talk. "Baby," I whispered. "Give me back my shoes."

Baby stared at me intensely as she whispered, "No."

"Listen," I said. "Taking my shoes won't stop me from going to work. I won't stop doing what I know how to do. As long as I'm giving you a hundred dollars a day, you can't touch me."

Baby pushed me. I put my hands behind my back and held them together. I needed to talk to Baby in a way she would understand. "If you think I'm going to put a hand on Prince's number one bottom bitch, you are wrong. I saw what happened to Essence for barely slapping you. No, sweetie, I'm not getting my ass whipped over you."

Baby said, "You will stop working these bullshit jobs because I'm the bitch in charge of you. You have been here for three months without taking a single customer. I'm telling you this because I'm your friend."

"Bitch, I ain't missed a payment yet." I took a breath and continued, "Do you think it is loyalty to you that stops me from telling Prince how badly Irish is doing? I know that you are taking in extra tricks to pretend like she is doing well. Her room shares a wall with me. I can hear her sobbing every single day. She prays to God for direction; then she goes out every night with you to turn tricks. You think I'm not telling

Prince because I'm afraid of you? You think I feel sorry for you or Irish? I don't. And I won't. You think I'm not telling Prince because I'm a kind woman? You think I'm still the bitch you can chase down and bring back to Prince? Listen to me; I am not that bitch anymore. Let me tell you the kind of bitch I am, the kind of bitch you have made me into. Give me my shoes or I will call Prince, tell him all the trouble you are having with Irish and make some new shit up. I plan to stay out of whoring as long as I possibly can. As for you being my friend, you do smile at me every day as I'm working my ass off around here. You bring me your take-out leftovers like I'm your dog. You try to show me kindness, but you will never be my friend. Now give me my shoes."

Baby reached under her covers and handed me my shoes. As she glared at me, she said, "I am going to fuck you up."

"You keep saying that, Baby. And I keep saying back to you, more than I already am?" I spat. "You are going to fuck me up more than I already fucked myself up? I don't think so."

I walked out of the room then and laughed as I closed the door. I walked away thinking about how badly I wanted to punch her in the nose. But I knew I would never hit her. I wanted to get away from this hell even more than I wanted to beat Baby's ass. The control that it took not to turn around and slap Baby in the face would serve me well later in life. Delayed gratification is a hard lesson to learn. Baby taught me that lesson well.

Life was getting ready to cut me a break.

Chapter 15
Slipping into Darkness

> "The only good luck many great men ever had was being born with the ability and determination to overcome bad luck." –Channing Pollock

I spent four months in darkness. Four months ducking and dodging trying not to be made into somebody's whore. Trying not to have someone taking pornographic pictures taken of me. Being in darkness is horrible. It's horrific to be around crazy, dishonest people for so long that things that are wrong start to seem normal to you. It's not normal to be dishonest, or to steal and manipulate. It's not normal to force another person to sell their body.

I put myself in a position in that house that made things a little easier for me. Because I was cleaning the house every day and cooking in the evenings, Baby allocated fifty dollars for me to take the clothes to be cleaned. I took over laundry from Baby, who had been spending that whole fifty bucks to do it, but I found a cheaper place so that I could skim four dollars a week off of the clothing chore.

I started getting an allowance for buying food, which was about fifteen bucks daily. Because I often took requests, the girls would slip in another extra five or ten when they wanted something in particular. I did what I could to find sales so that I could put another couple of bucks into my pocket, sometimes.

I was essentially the personal assistant for all three of them. I picked up the clothes they left around the house and I washed them. I cleaned the house. I picked up their dry cleaning. I combed their hair. I bought the soap. I took messages and made appointments for them. In addition to all of that, I was still working every day doing specimen collections and the factory assembly jobs.

I was also busily causing trouble in small ways because nobody expected me to cause trouble. I would do these innocent little things that nobody would think I had done, let alone intentionally, to cause trouble. I remember one time I bought a really sweet watermelon so that everybody could have a piece. It was delicious, and we had some left over, so I said I was going to wrap up a section for each person and put them in the refrigerator. I made sure the watermelon would be there when they came home after their night of turning tricks. They would each have a slice of delicious watermelon to eat at the end of their long night. So, I wrapped up two pieces and put them in the fridge. Before I wrapped up the third piece, I took a big bite right out of the middle. And then I wrapped that one up as well and put it in the refrigerator with the others.

When the ladies came in that night, I could hear the fight break out in the kitchen because one of them felt somebody—one of the three of them—had taken a bite out of the middle of their watermelon. Of course, they hadn't. They didn't even consider that it had been me, but this led to a fight that was so vicious they had to get Prince involved.

In addition to all the other things I did for the girls, I also made up something I called booty-call kits. Booty-call kits were these little plastic bags I would fill with things they could use to freshen themselves up after a trick. I put some ChapStick, clean panties, a damp cloth inside a separate plastic bag, and a couple of Life Savers for them. They would put those little kits in their purse, and it made them feel fresh. It was little things like that that helped them still feel human.

But sometimes I would deliberately put out only two kits instead of three, because what would happen if there were only two kits. I would put the kits out and they'd each pick one up as they were headed out the door. Someone would always think that one of the other ladies had taken two kits, which would cause another eruption of fights. I didn't help to resolve these fights either, because when they would ask me how many I put out my answer was always the same: three. I insisted that I put out one for everyone as I got the missing kit out so that everyone had one. In such a dark period of my life, I got my thrills where I could, and these little acts of aggression made me feel invincible. I was planning my escape in any way that I could. The same way that when you are on an airplane and it drops a few feet, you start to look around to the exits so that if something happened, you knew what to do. You check out the closest exit. My thinking was to wait for my chance and have an executable plan.

In the midst of that, about two weeks after Irish ran away the first time, Essence disappeared. She just took off. They took her out to do her tricks and she didn't come back at the end of the night. She turned up four days later, and it turned out that she had met up with a john who had a seemingly endless supply of drugs. She went with that person until the drugs ran out. To punish Essence, they didn't beat her with the stick or put her in the van. What they did was stop giving her pictures or reports on her son and that broke her down. She didn't run away again for a long time after that.

The key for me was that I needed to pretend as if I cared about these girls, so acts of kindness counted. An extra piece of chicken for one. Picking up their clothes early for another. Waking them up or helping them do their hair. Helping them rub their back or rub oil on their skin. All those little acts of kindness made sure they trusted me and wanted me around, at least until Irish started acting right.

I would also attempt to sabotage Irish as much as I could to make sure she never got on track, but I knew that one day she would get it and the moment that happened I would be the new trainee. The fact of the matter was that I was simply waiting for a chance to get the hell out. My problem was Prince. As long as Prince was able to follow me, he might make good on all those threats he had made to myself and my family. I needed an opportunity to get out where he couldn't follow me. I was waiting for that chance to come along, and I would take it and I would not look back for one second.

The key was that I was working in the nursing homes. I was working on the assembly lines. I was the personal assistant to all the women. I was cooking, cleaning, washing, and doing booty-call kits—and I was glad to be doing that instead of having to perform escort services. I was watching Irish get beat down. It was only a matter of time until Irish did what they wanted her to do. It was sad and disheartening. I needed a chance. I only needed one chance to get out of there and back to Chicago where my dad could protect me, but I still needed a way that Prince couldn't follow me. When that moment showed itself, I would take it without hesitation.

Chapter 16
Stick Me with a Fork

"If opportunity doesn't knock, build a door."*—
Milton Berle

My last day at Tara I woke to a lot of chaos in the house. We're talking significant hullabaloo. The women were running around like crazy. I woke up to Baby at my door screaming at me to get up. It was about three in the morning; I wasn't up yet. I would typically get up around five because that's when the ladies would come in.

I got up and made my way out of my room to where I find out that Prince has been arrested. He's been charged with the rape of his best friend's girlfriend. I was shocked, but I believed he did it. My reasoning behind that belief was because I knew that Prince considered himself to be irresistible. He thought every woman wanted him. And if his best friend's girlfriend didn't want him, then I am certain that he would have tried to show her what he had to make sure she knew that she wanted him.

Since Prince was charged with rape, he had been arrested and picked up. He was going to be arraigned in the morning. Baby was going to the arraignment and was insisting that I go with her. We got up, got dressed, and went down to the courthouse. When you're dealing with criminal court, there is no published schedule. We got there about eight-thirty in the morning and his case came up at around noon. He plead not guilty and his bail was set at $250,000 due to prior offenses. We needed to get our hands on $25,000 (10 percent) to bond him out.

We went to a few bondsmen but found that no bondsman would help due to his prior offenses and the fact that bondsmen had to hunt him down before when they had put up money for him. We eventually gave up with the bondsmen and headed back to Tara. Once we got home, Baby admitted that there was enough money at Prince's house to bond him out. She would need to go in the safe to get the cash and then bring it back. One of us would go down, bail him out, and bring him back to Tara.

While Baby was gone, I made clear to everyone that I did not want to be the one to go down to the jail. I told them I thought that somebody who knew the jail system should go down there. I insisted I should not be the one to go because I didn't have any prior offenses, they didn't know anything about me, and I didn't want my name on anything associated with Prince.

When Baby got back, she then insisted that I was the only one who could go down to the jail. Apparently, she thought the police were looking for all of them. Of course, I didn't want to go to the jail. I wanted to stay in the house, but Baby being Baby. . . she wrapped up the cash, put it in a bag, handed me my purse, told me to get the hell out and go get Prince. She told me to take the car and go.

I took the car and left. I got in and drove straight to the airport. I did not go to the jail, and never had any intention of bailing Prince out. I didn't have anything with me but the clothes I was wearing, my purse, and the twenty-five grand. I bought an airline ticket to Chicago. I got on a plane, and I went home.

When I got to Chicago, I took a cab to my mom's house. I walked up the steps, knocked on the door, and rang the bell—desperate to be with my family again. My sister opened the door with my son on her hip. My son reached out for me and hugged me around my neck. I walked back into the protection of my mom and my dad—into the comfort of my family. I was elated because I knew that Prince wasn't going to get out of jail unless Baby had another huge stash of money somewhere. Maybe Prince did, but I didn't think Baby would have had access to it.

I admit that was treachery. I took the bail money. I did not look back, and I did not care. I had been in darkness for months, and that was far too long. It was only by the luck of having Irish doing so poorly that I never ended up being somebody's whore. I guess you could call that the luck of the Irish.

I found it remarkable that I knew that no one would leave with me. I didn't even ask them, and I can also tell you why I didn't ask them. You know how the circus does it when they train an elephant? They take a baby elephant and tie them to a stake. The baby elephant can't pull the stake out, and it learns pretty quickly it's not strong enough to escape. That lesson stays with the baby elephant as it grows up, and the grown elephant doesn't even attempt to pull the stake out. That is the how Prince had these girls trained—all of them. They were convinced that trying to escape him was impossible, that they didn't have the strength to pull the stake out and run away. Prince would always find them and bring them back. But Prince couldn't find anyone and bring them back if he was in jail.

The elephant training hadn't taken with me. I knew damn well that as a grown elephant I could pull the stake out. And the second I got the chance, I did. Once I got back to Chicago, I sent Essence the address of the kids. I made it look like a letter from a trick with the return address being the address of the ghetto daycare Prince had tried to force me to keep Shawn in. About six weeks later, I got a phone call from Baby telling me that they were ready for me to come back and that all was forgiven. I thought to myself, *Bite me, I'm not going back there. Not for a second. Not for a moment. Not for a minute."* But I saved my breath just like I saved myself. I simply told her, "No."

Chapter 17
Where Are They Now?

> "See when you drive home today, you've got a big windshield on the front of your car. And you've got a little bitty rearview mirror. And the reason the windshield is so large, and the rearview mirror is so small is because what's happened in your past is not near as important as what's in your future."
> —Joel Osteen

Prince did not escape punishment for the rape. He was guilty. The ladies never got Prince out on bail either. He remained at the county jail until his trial. He was found guilty of rape and sentenced to ten years in prison. I thought those three girls, with the help of the streetwalkers, could have made that bail money quickly, but they were unprotected. Without Prince there, there's no telling what happened to them.

He raped his best friend's girl because he wanted her, and she didn't want him. The fact that he had four women he could rape with impunity did not matter. In his mind, he could have anyone he wanted. He was superior to his old friend, so why couldn't he have sex with his woman. He spent three years in jail and was released early for good behavior. Baby was there when Prince was released. She located me in Chicago and asked me to come back. I refused. I don't know what happened to them after that.

Essence, despite her best efforts and her stunning beauty, ended up a cheap crack whore. She was unable to overcome the terrible atrocities that happened to her as a young girl. The repeated abuse and rape as a child destroyed any sense of self-worth she may have once had. I don't know what happened to her child.

Irish returned to Ireland but kept turning tricks. She was never heard from again.

As for me, I went back home and continued with my crazy behavior another few years before eventually returning to school for my electrical engineering degree, master's degree, and more. I was honored numerous times over the years and received, among other accolades, the New York YMCA Leadership award.

The car stopped moving. I snapped out of my reminiscing. As the driver hopped out of the car to let me out, I double-checked that he had the address to deliver my bags. I was staying at the company apartment while I was in town.

As I walked into the skyscraper, I thought how strange it was to be back in Cleveland. What would I be doing now if I had not had the smarts to escape? Would I even be alive? My adventure with Prince and the ladies set me up for success. Hard work has never deterred me. The skills of observation and negotiation have served me well. I know not to take things at face value. The ability to empathize when needed but to be ruthless as required made a difference to my corporate success. I escaped a well-set trap that has been used on young women for countless years. The trap was thought to be foolproof; it was not. Remember, there is no trap or circumstance that is inescapable. It took a combination of planning, preparation, backbreaking work, and a bit of chance to create the opportunity to change my destiny.

If I can do it, anyone can. If I can escape an inescapable trap, anyone can. Start now.

Caged Bird

A free bird leaps
on the back of the wind
and floats downstream
till the current ends
and dips his wing
in the orange sun rays
and dares to claim the sky.

But a bird that stalks
down his narrow cage
can seldom see through
his bars of rage
his wings are clipped and
his feet are tied
so he opens his throat to sing.

The caged bird sings
with a fearful trill
of things unknown
but longed for still
and his tune is heard
on the distant hill
for the caged bird
sings of freedom

The free bird thinks of another breeze
and the trade winds soft through the signing trees

and the fat worms waiting on a dawn bright lawn
and he names the sky his own

But a caged bird stands on the grave of dreams
his shadow shouts on a nightmare scream
his wings are clipped and his feet are tied

so he opens his throat to sing.

The caged bird sings
with a fearful trill
of things unknown
but longed for still
and his tune is heard
on the distant hill
for the caged bird
sings of freedom.
Maya Angelou, Caged Bird

Visualize this thing you want. See it, feel it, believe in it. Make your mental blueprint and begin to build.

Robert Collier

First of all, thank you so much for buying and reading my first book, *NEVER a $7 Whore*. I know that everyone is busy. You could have spent your time doing anything else, but you chose to read my book. For that, I am extremely grateful.

I hope that my narrative provided some relief from your daily grind; if so, I would appreciate it if you would share this book with someone else. No one is perfect—if you enjoyed my book (or if you didn't), I would like to hear from you at my website, tonicrowewriter.com. If you enjoyed the book, please write a review for me at Amazon.com. Reviews on Amazon help new writers immensely. Just click on the review area where the stars are and start your book review there.

Your feedback can only help this new writer improve. Thank you up front for any feedback you are willing to provide to me. Feedback will allow me to improve my writing. I hope you have a great day.

Toni Crowe, The Writer.

ACKNOWLEDGMENTS

Since he found out many years ago that I love to write (and that I ran away with a pimp!), my husband, Bill, has been urging me to write my story down. It became a running joke in our family, including with my children, Sean and Tamara. "Mom," they would say, "when are you going to write the 'I could have been a $7 wh*re story?" I would smile and tell them, "One day." Recently, Bill pointed out that I had both an unusual university experience and corporate career that were part of my story. I, of course, continued to talk about "one day." Well, "one day" is now.

I could not have completed this book without the support of my family and friends.

My sisters, Rhoda and Van, kept me on the straight and narrow. Human memory is a fragile thing. My sisters kept me focused on the truth.

My best friend for life, Karen, sister of my heart and speaker of wisdom, thank you for being my friend.

My big dysfunctional family for all of the support you provided at critical stages.

My ride-or-die girls: Janlaw, Deb, Donna, and Pat—

your insights and help made a difference in the final quality of the book.

And finally, my technical support, and husband. I would never have written this book without your urging. The support you provided was priceless. All the social media and landing pages, and SEO data, etc., etc., was invaluable, but more than that you believed in me. That more than anything made this book happen.

I love you all, and I could not have done this without you.

Do you want to know what happened to Baby?

Writing this book made me want to know what happened to each of the ladies.

I took the time to find out.

If you want to know what happened to Baby after I left Tara, go to the link below.

Baby got everything she deserved.

Being "Bottom Bitch" is a tough job. You have to use both carrots and sticks to keep your ladies in line.

Baby had it down to a science, using cruelty and kindness to control. Throughout my time at Tara, Baby made my life hell, yet she also showed moments of great empathy.

Use the link below and I will send you my true-crime short story, "What Happened to Baby?"

http://www.tonicrowewriter.com/thank-you-for-reading-my-book-back-page/

BULLETS and BOSSES DON'T HAVE FRIENDS:
How to Navigate Tough Challenges in the Workplace

Don't know if you have what it takes to make it in the corporate world?

Learn practical strategies from a black belt in business now!

Buy Now!

https://www.amazon.com/dp/B07JH6W8XH

If you enjoyed Never A $7 Wh*re,
would you leave me a honest review on Amazon.com?

Amazon uses reviews as one of the parameters to rank books and determines how much marketing help they will provide.

I would appreciate an honest review at:
https://www.amazon.com/dp/B07G5Q2GV5

ABOUT THE AUTHOR

Toni Crowe was born to her fifteen-year-old mother on Chicago's tough West Side. Her mom met and married her dad when she was five. He eventually moved the family to Chicago's South Side. She became pregnant with her first child, giving birth at fifteen like her mother. Despite the birth, Toni graduated with her class from Lindblom Technical High School at sixteen. She was enrolled in a Welfare to Work (CETA) program at a doctor's office, where she was taught to be a medical assistant. It was this job she left to run off with a pimp.

After returning to Chicago, Toni did not immediately settle down. She had her second child at twenty-one, again applying for welfare and again being put into a Welfare to Work program. Toni became a state-certified laboratory assistant. Her grandmother, Vandella, interceded with Toni in a determined and robust fashion, causing an epiphany that forced Toni down the right track. Toni applied to the University of Illinois-Chicago, eventually graduating with a degree in engineering.

After obtaining employment at a major aircraft and missile manufacturer, Toni obtained her master's degree in organizational management, became a professional engineer in Wisconsin, and a certified professional manager. Toni learned Lean Manufacturing at a Fortune 500 company, including intense training in Japan. Later, Toni became a certified designer for Six Sigma Green Belt and commandeered a Six Sigma Leadership Black Belt. Each of these facilitated her climb up the corporate ladder. Toni has served on a number of nonprofit boards and believes in giving back to the community. Toni has been happily married for many years. She is now chasing her dream of being a multi-book published author.

Contact Toni via her website, tonicrowewriter.com.

Made in the USA
Lexington, KY
02 December 2018